The Library Reference Series

LIBRARY HISTORY AND BIOGRAPHY

The Library Reference Series

Lee Ash

General Editor

AMERICAN LIBRARY PIONEERS
II

Samuel Swett Green

By
ROBERT KENDALL SHAW

GREGG PRESS
Boston   1972

This is a complete photographic reprint of a work
first published in Chicago by the American Library Association in 1926.

First Gregg Press edition published 1972.

Printed on permanent/durable acid-free paper in
The United States of America.

Library of Congress Cataloging in Publication Data

Shaw, Robert Kendall, 1871-
   Samuel Swett Green.

   (Library reference series)
   Reprint of the 1926 ed., issued in series: American
library pioneers, no. 2.
   Bibliography: p. 83-86.
   1. Green, Samuel Swett, 1837-1918. I. Title.
Z720.G8S5 1972   020'.92'4   72-8743
ISBN 0-8398-1885-8

AMERICAN LIBRARY PIONEERS

ARTHUR E. BOSTWICK
EDITOR

II
Samuel Swett Green

Samuel S. Green.

Samuel Swett Green

BY

ROBERT KENDALL SHAW

LIBRARIAN, WORCESTER PUBLIC LIBRARY

Chicago

AMERICAN LIBRARY ASSOCIATION

1926

D. B. UPDIKE, THE MERRYMOUNT PRESS, BOSTON

CONTENTS

ILLUSTRATIONS

Samuel Swett Green

SAMUEL SWETT GREEN

CHAPTER I

DAWN — SUNRISE

*There is no city so great or renowned that does not wear
its library as the chief jewel in its crown.* GEORGE F. HOAR

THE library atmosphere surrounding these
United States at the birth of Samuel S. Green
was much more invigorating locally than nationally. The pleasant little farming village of Worcester, with its 5000-odd inhabitants just rubbing their
eyes to the new dawn of coming industrialism, in the
last year of the reign of Andrew Jackson was by no
means a library Sahara. The Worcester "Lyceum"
which, according to authentic local history, was "possessed of a well-selected library of about 500 volumes,
beneficially and extensively used by the young artisans
of this village," was in 1837, the year of Mr. Green's
birth, a lusty infant, aged eight, while the American
Antiquarian Society (and library), the brightest and
oldest jewel in Worcester's literary crown, in the
course of the same year, completed its first quarter-
century. It was the attraction of the latter library
that in this same 1837 brought the "Learned Blacksmith," Elihu Burritt, to Worcester, on account of
the wealth of its philological treasures.

Mr. Burritt is said to have walked into Worcester

from his native New Britain, Connecticut, with all
his earthly possessions tied up in the traditional ban-
dana handkerchief; at any rate it was with scanty resources, but a burning zeal for humanity, that he
arrived here and set to work as a blacksmith, sparing
what time he could find for his beloved grammars and
dictionaries at the "Antiquarian Hall." It is a melancholy tradition in Worcester, in view of Mr. Burritt's
shining example as a savior of odd moments by his
habit of holding a Hebrew grammar in one hand and
blowing the bellows with the other, or of storing a
Greek text in his tall hat, while standing at the forge,
that with all his intellectual zeal, he remained a poor
blacksmith.

It was but two years before, in 1835, that the tragic
upset of a stage-coach in Ohio cut short the career
of Worcester's most ardent and successful early librarian, Christopher Columbus Baldwin, whose intel-
ligent zeal as a collector and organizer raised the
rapidly growing library of the American Antiquarian
Society to a national and well-deserved prominence.

Within the limits of this same decade, in 1831,
closed the long life of the patriot-publisher, Isaiah
Thomas, who brought his printing-press to Worcester
on the eve of the battle of Lexington, and continued
his successful career here as printer and patron of
learning during more than half a century. It was he
who in 1812 founded the American Antiquarian
Society, bequeathing, in addition to a site and hall,

his valuable library of eight thousand volumes, and a liberal fund for maintenance.

The year 1831 also marks a plain and early milestone in Worcester's industrial life, as the motorist, speeding northward out Grove Street today, may note that date carved in granite on the oldest wire-mill now forming a unit of the American Steel and Wire Company.

Nationally, on the other hand, the library atmosphere was thin and unstimulating. In February, 1837, the month of Mr. Green's birth, "Old Hickory" was preparing, at last, to lay down the big stick which he had wielded so stoutly, to the dismay of conservatives, during two stormy and despotic administrations. How friendly an ear President Jackson would have lent to the modest requests of library trustees is perhaps not too conjectural; but certainly no president, before or since, has thrust himself up to his high position with as little help from the printed page as the hero of New Orleans.

For the first time a plain, rugged man of the people had forced his way to the presidency, practically unassisted by education, formal or informal, of any kind. Writing and spelling he dreaded, to the end of his life, vastly more than a pointed pistol, and his ignorance on many matters of ordinary knowledge was colossal. With the intellectual types of Lincoln or Garfield he had little in common. The contrast with the scholarly statesmanship of the two Adamses,

[5]

Jefferson and Madison was immense. Sheer force of character, accompanied by honesty and determination, was shown for once to be sufficient qualification for the highest office in the gift of the people.

As Jackson was essentially a product of his time, it follows that the same low regard for education, whether through the formal avenue of the college, or the people's university, the library, was generally current during the Jacksonian era, to be followed presently by the intellectual revival, led by Longfellow, Lowell, Prescott, Bancroft and other writers of first rank.

Mr. Green's family has resided in or near Worcester for over two hundred years, his great-great-grandfather, Dr. Thomas Green, having moved in 1717, at the age of eighteen, to Leicester from Malden, with his father Samuel. Leicester is a charming hill-town, adjoining Worcester, and there, in his new home, tradition has it that the youthful Thomas met two English ship-surgeons (said to have been pardoned buccaneers) who turned his active mind to the study of medicine. A more prosy legend ascribes Thomas's first interest in the healing art to the chance perusal of a medical book in his father's library. The lad also established friendly relations with the Indian doctors in the neighborhood, and learned from them such herbal lore as they possessed.

This Dr. Thomas Green (1699–1773) must have been a man of extraordinary energy as well as ability, for not only was he a successful country practitioner (said to have taught 123 medical students during his long career), but he also turned preacher, joining the Baptist Church, and in 1737 was ordained co-pastor at Sutton.

At a Leicester church anniversary some forty years ago the Rev. Hiram C. Estes said of this physician of soul and body: "Dr. Green lived three lives and did the work of three men in one: he was a man of business, active, energetic and successful; he was also a noted physician, and a preacher of the Gospel, quite as eminent in this as in his other spheres of life."

Speaking of the Green family in general, we may note that, in its local history, Worcester is fortunate in the existence of a little book of quaint and original literary flavor, entitled *Carl's Tour in Main Street* and originally contributed to a local newspaper about 1855. One of the joint authors supplied the facts from his ample store of memory, while the other clothed them in a picturesque and literary form. For certain more detailed and pointed facts about the Green family than the following quotation, the reader is referred to the book itself:

I have no authority for this statement; but the supposition is my own that the young man Thomas Green went out from his father's house, carrying with him his medical library of one volume, that he might associate with the Indians enough to obtain from them their secret of curing diseases; as in the early days of this country, medical men were glad to avail themselves of every means within their reach for enlarging their ability to heal the sick. The young Dr. Thomas Green strolled away a two days' journey at least from the house of his childhood, till he came to a shelving rock that formed a sort of cave near a spring of pure water that bubbled out of "Strawberry Bank"—now Leicester Hill—where, like the modern philosopher of Walden Pond, he took up his abode; nature his teacher, the green earth his bed, the blue sky his covering, and the wild men of the forest his only neighbors. There was something more than romance in that. There was stern reality. The medical philosopher became devout under the teachings of nature; and as society gathered itself around him, the settlers looked to the man Thomas for medicine for the mind as well as for the body. He became a preacher as well as a doctor. He gathered a church, a Baptist church; preached on Sundays and practised physic on week-days.

Time went on; and when the preacher-doctor had reached nearly the middle point allotted as the life of man, there was born to him a son whom he named John, probably because it was the name borne by that disciple whom Jesus loved. The boy John was early initiated into the mysteries of the healing art, and as soon as he had reached his majority, he quitted the paternal roof at "Strawberry Bank," and, following down the course of Kettle Brook, he took up his abode in Worcester, nearly four-score years anterior to the time when my father and I passed by the house of his worthy descendant

(which is again almost another four-score before the penciling of these pages).

It was as ministers to bodily, rather than spiritual needs, however, that so many members of the Green family, both in and out of Worcester, were to find reputation and success during five generations. Dr. Thomas's son, the first John Green, moved to Worcester, on coming of age, and settled at the north end of town on a handsome estate of five hundred acres, known for generations as "Green Hill" and recently acquired by the City of Worcester as a public park.

Dr. John Green, second, died, in 1808, at the early age of forty-five. He had practiced, however, for twenty-seven years, and during the last nine was practically the only physician in town. The *Worcester Spy* reported that "To his funeral came the largest concourse of people from this and neighboring towns ever known to be collected here on a similar occasion."

Of two brothers in the next generation it seems proper to speak in this place: the oldest son, John, the benefactor of the Worcester Public Library, and the fifth son, James, the father of the subject of this biography.

Dr. John Green, third Worcester physician of the name, in direct line, graduated from Brown University in 1804, and began the practice of medicine in Worcester three years later. This practice he continued steadily for almost half a century, retiring, on account of failing health, in 1855. About 1815 he also started, in addition to his growing practice of medicine, and in order to exercise a proper supervision over his prescriptions, the apothecary's business which his younger brother James afterward followed with

so much success. Having early decided to devote a
liberal sum to the foundation of a free library for
his native town, he was engaged during many years
in the assembling of an excellent nucleus for a reference library, rich in literature and theology, which
exceeded eight thousand volumes at his death in 1865.

Dr. Green's chief legacy of $30,000 was remarkable
for its generosity and especially for the wise provision attached to the gift: that one-fourth of the income should be added to the principal, until the fund
should equal $100,000. For nearly sixty years, there-
fore, the good people of Worcester have been enjoying that rare privilege of "eating their cake and having it too," the income from this fund available for
the purchase of books being now some $3500 an-
nually, while Dr. Green's original $30,000 of 1859
exceeds $71,000.

How close the future public library was to Dr.
Green's heart may be seen from a perusal of his will,
in which all matters of detail are wisely and carefully
planned. With how little accuracy, on the other hand,
the philanthropist of 1859 could forecast the extent of
the library movement of the twentieth century, one
may note from a clause of the will looking to provision for the Circulation as well as the Reference Department.

Referring to his plans as embodied in his will, Dr.
Green states that eventually there will be "a residuum of income to be applied to the circulating or

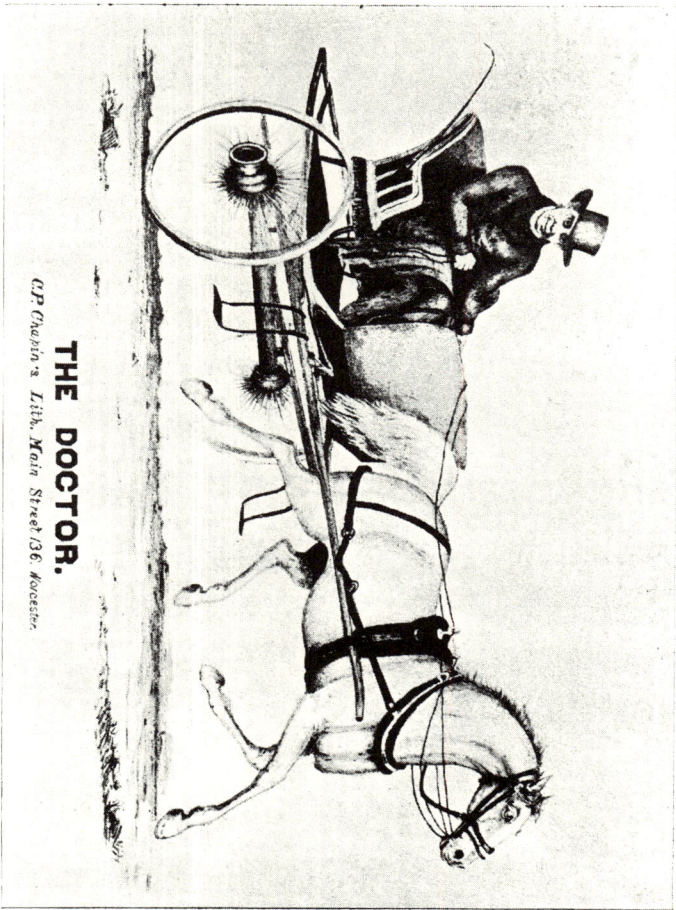

THE DOCTOR.

C.P Chapin's Lith. Main Street 136. Worcester.

JOHN GREEN, 3ᴰ, 1784–1865

lending department, which residuum will be constantly increasing, and which at some future day will probably be sufficient to meet all the wants of the said circulating or lending department, and to relieve the city altogether of the expenses of an institution which, I trust, will be an ornament and a blessing to the community for whose welfare it has been established"!

James Green, father of Samuel the librarian, was but six years old when his father died, and had to go to work early for a living, enjoying practically no schooling after the age of twelve. Feeling keenly this lack of formal education, he was determined to do the very best for his children, and saw to it that his three sons all went through Harvard College and secured the best possible professional education as well. For many years Mr. James Green conducted an apothecary's business, which practically expanded to the size of a "general store," at different places on Main Street, until his death in 1874. The labor and sacrifice necessary for the task of providing so thorough an education for three sons, besides bringing up a daughter, and all without any financial aid or support beyond his own efforts and those of his devoted wife, speak volumes for the character of the man.

Mrs. James Green was a woman of great personal charm and social gifts. She survived her husband many years, until the opening of the present century. The daughter of Samuel Swett of Boston and Dedham, this Elizabeth Swett Green could trace her descent through her mother, daughter of Dr. John Sprague of Boston, to an even earlier resident of Massachusetts Bay Colony than Thomas Green, that is, Ralph Sprague, who came to Charlestown in 1629 from Upway, Devonshire, England.

A maternal ancestor to whom Mr. Green must have pointed with just pride was Rev. John Woodbridge, one of the earliest settlers of Newbury, and brother of Dr. Benjamin Woodbridge whose name stands first in the Harvard Quinquennial Catalogue, in the premier class of 1642.

The old brick house in which Mr. Green was born on Monday, February 20, 1837, still stands on School Street, though debased to commercial uses. Modern industrialism has played havoc, residentially speaking, with that quarter of the town, for wherever, as in New England, the prevailing fair winds are westerly, smoke from factories is regularly driven eastward, creating in most of our manufacturing cities an east side unsuitable for residential purposes.

No untoward events seem to have disturbed Worcester's village tranquillity at this midwinter period. The financial storm-cloud of 1837, induced by the wildcat speculation of the Jacksonian epoch, was still no bigger than a man's hand on the western horizon. In the local *Massachusetts Spy* for February 22, James Green advertises calmly six tons of copperas just received, to be sold on favorable terms;

also a fresh supply of indelible (two *l*'s in the text and one in the caption) ink, English and American, but with no hint of any added paternal pride over the birth of a second son.

Among the other advertisements noted on the same generous folio sheet, are that of that infant prodigy, two years old, the Boston and Worcester Railroad, running two trains daily each way (fare $2 as compared with $1.60 in 1926); also of its ancient rival, the stage-coach, taking passengers to Norwich in time for the New York boat, which, *D. V.*, might hope to land them in the metropolis after a twenty-two hours' voyage (tickets $5). Perhaps a librarian's vocation for baby Sam is vaguely foreshadowed by Dow and Howland's notice, on this same front page, of their desire to sell *Dick on Covetousness; Mammon* by Rev. J. Harris; *The Young Lady's Friend; A Poor Rich Man; The Young Bride at Home,* etc.

A shy and quiet little fellow, always more devoted to study and other indoor pursuits than to playing with companions in the neighborhood, our future librarian began his formal education, at a very tender age, in Mrs. Levi Heywood's infant school. Following a tradition mentioned by Mr. Green himself in an illuminating paper printed in the *Library Journal* for December, 1913, we learn that, though very young to go to school, he was tremendously desirous of doing what his big brother did.

A novel pedagogical theory advanced and practiced by Mrs. Heywood provided that, when children misbehave, they are not naughty, but fatigued, and consequently several spare beds were prepared in a back room for the accommodation of recalcitrants. Severe cases were undressed and put to bed, with drawn curtains. One queries if that were not rather a transfer than a triumph of discipline.

His next school, however, kept by Mrs. Sarah B. Wood, was a more important educational factor, as he remained there for several years, and also was there first introduced to libraries of a public character. Not only the Worcester Lyceum's books, previously mentioned, but also the Bangs Library (belonging to Mr. Green's Unitarian parish) were shelved in Mrs. Wood's schoolroom. "Saturday afternoons the furniture of the schoolroom was rearranged, and Mrs. Wood stood behind a barrier, in immaculately clean and tastefully trimmed cap, and a spare gown, and dispensed and charged books."

Creatures of environment we must all become to some extent, and who can say that the youthful Samuel, even at that tender age, confronted by a library and school together in the same room, may not have absorbed some adumbration of an idea of potential cooperation between those two basic educational agencies? Was he not perhaps drawing a dual inspiration from his environment so that, when the clarion of '76 should summon him to battle for the cause of free libraries, he too, like his prototype of the Old Testament, might be ready with his fervent answer, "Here am I"?

From Mrs. Wood's fostering care, young Samuel was promoted in due course to the public grammar school. The examination which he had to pass was oral and, being conducted by his kindly and genial pastor, whose face and manners were familiar, was much less of an ordeal than might be expected. "Everything went smoothly in these upper grades," says Mr. Green. "I did especially well in arithmetic, and gained rapid promotion on that account. Parsing I did not comprehend there, but as my mind developed, and the study of Latin was begun in the High School, I became fond of grammar. My standing was always good in the latter school, which I entered at the age of twelve, and where I remained until I went to Harvard College at the age of seventeen, in 1854."

Before proceeding further with this sketch, the reader should note a home influence of great sweetness and of highest importance throughout sixty years of Mr. Green's life.

Brought up by my mother mainly, I was always treated with the greatest tenderness. It must have been easy to govern me, for if I had done anything wrong, all that she had to do was to express her disapproval by looking sober. I could not bear being estranged from my mother for more than a few minutes, and was ready to submit my will to hers because of the necessity which I felt for being in sympathy with her. I do not think that she ever dreamed of striking me or of asking my father to do so. This intimacy and mutual affection lasted through life. I gave up marriage, and when she was left alone, took care of her until she died, in her ninety-fourth year. Her last words, and I think I have never spoken of this before, were "Sam, I love you dearly."

Could filial duty expect any higher reward? Another strong ethical motive was self-respect and a desire to appear well in the sight of those whom he loved.

For all this sweet mutual relation between mother and son, Mr. Green himself believed that his mother's method of permitting him to stay indoors with her rather than to be playing in the neighborhood, as a normal little boy should, was hardly wise, in the long run. At any rate, he grew up a delicate child and remained subject to frequent attacks by various illnesses till long past early manhood. In fact, he belonged to that rather unusual type whose health steadily improved as he grew older; he says himself that he had his last illness in 1870 (at the age of thirty-three), and although that statement can no longer be true, it was made as late as 1913. Certainly the Worcester library's memory, which now dates back thirty-four years, recalls no instance of his ever missing an hour from the library on account of ill health.

As a proof of too much "domesticity," Mr. Green preserved till the close of his life certain pieces of worsted embroidery made by his older brother and himself. He admits that the amount of outdoor life and exercise that he received were wholly insufficient, and that, during his college course and for several years after graduation, he was much of an invalid.

Probably as an extract from his personal diary, Mr. Green caused to be printed, under the caption "My First Play" a vital bit of local history of 1847.

I recollect distinctly that while walking along Main Street one day soon after I was ten years old, my attention was riveted by a show-bill fastened to the front of the Central Hotel, which stood on the site of the present Bay State House. The placard was very large, much larger than we were in the habit of seeing in Worcester at that time; the print was of unusual size, too. I remember well the amazement with which I read the announcement that several excellent plays including *The Hunchback* would be staged at the "National Athenaeum" (parquettee, 50c.; settees, 25c.); Brinley Hall was to be the "National Athenaeum" for a few weeks.

My uncle, the late Dr. John Green, founder of the Free Public Library, was very fond of theatrical performances, and one of their leading and constant patrons in Worcester. Consider my delight when he invited me to accompany him to see the play of *Douglas*. My imagination had been stirred by the sight of the great show-bill, and my mind was full of pleasant anticipations. Going with Dr. Green to Brinley Hall, we were conducted to the front portion of the hall, to seats in the parquette, just before the stage and occupied by a few rows of hair-cloth sofas. Settees filled the main body of the hall.

The play of *Douglas* made a profound impression upon me. The stage was small; the scenery undoubtedly inadequate. These things did not trouble me, however, for I knew nothing about the grand effects which can be produced on a large stage, well provided with scenic and other appointments. Everything was fine in my eyes. I have no doubt that the acting was good. . . . The names of the actors [W. H. Smith, E. F. Keach, Miss Gann] also show that the company was a strong one.

I shall always remember the delightful sensations and thoughts which I had when young Norval first came upon the stage, and, to give information regarding himself, recited the lines beginning:

> "*My name is Norval, on the Grampian hills*
> *My father feeds his flocks.*"

There was a strong prejudice against theatrical performances in Worcester at the time when the company of which I have been writing came here. Perhaps my conscience was tenderer at that time than it is now; certain it is that it was less enlightened. At any rate, although I had been brought up in a family of liberal theological views, I remember that then or soon after I had serious doubts as to whether I ought to go to the theater. A very large proportion of the better class of Worcester people frowned upon public theatrical entertainments in 1847.

From all of which the reader may infer that Unitarian thought in Worcester eighty years ago was as liberal and progressive as it is today.

SAMUEL SWETT GREEN
at 21

CHAPTER II

MORNING

DURING his college years Mr. Green's indoor habits of life certainly marred, but did not really jeopardize, his career. After being at Cambridge for about a month he learned, to his great surprise, that he was rated at the head of his class. As he was suffering, however, from inflamed eyes at that time, he believed it would be an unwarrantable strain to try to maintain any such record, and therefore withdrew entirely for a few weeks' rest, and never tried to regain his former primacy. In spite of bad general health and worse eyesight, he finished his course pleasantly and profitably, keeping much to himself, and forming few friendships.

Among his Harvard classmates of 1858 were Winslow Warren, Henry P. Walcott, George A. Wentworth, Senator Pasco of Florida, and the famously "educated" Henry Adams. His two Worcester classmates from the local high school were Eugene F. Bliss, later a resident of Cincinnati, and Thomas Jefferson Spurr, mortally wounded at Antietam. Two others whose careers were definitely associated with Worcester, after college days, were George E. Francis, practicing physician for many years, and Joseph A. Shaw, for nearly forty years headmaster at Highland Military Academy. John L. Gardner, whose widow's art collections have brought to Boston so much fame, was also a member of this class. In 1870 Mr. Green's Alma Mater conferred on him the degree of M.A., and seven years later the Harvard chapter of Phi Beta Kappa elected him an honorary member.

To wind up now the valetudinary phase: Mr. Green described himself as "languid for two or three years after graduation." Failing to recover his health or to get definitely interested in anything, he undertook a long sailing voyage to Smyrna, in the summer of 1859, in the barque "Racehorse." Thence he continued by steamer to Constantinople and back to the former port in time to sail for home again in the same vessel. But the work of healing was not yet done. In the autumn of 1860 he entered the Harvard Divinity School, whither his natural love of religious, philosophical and historical study almost instinctively beckoned him. Within a month or so, however, his doctor sent him home, bidding him get a horse and ride around among the White Mountains. Although no record has been found of the purchase of the horse, the student's health improved so that he was able to enter the next class and graduate, without serious loss of time, in 1864.

In the school I found much benefit from the knowledge I gained of the principles of exegesis, and from the tussle I had with the great question of religious philosophy. My studies quieted my mind which had been troubled for years by inability to find solutions of great questions, and contributed powerfully to the restoration to excellent health afterward attained, and gave me a side-study, which has added, during all my life, to the enjoyment of active pursuits. When I left the Divinity School, I saw at once that my theology was unsalable, although today it would be regarded with quite general favor.

During the next five or six years, poor health pursued him more or less, but after that he enjoyed forty-five years of remarkable immunity from physical ailments.

Mr. Green's good health in middle and later years he justly attributed to the proper observance of the laws of health. Abstemious in diet to a fault, he carried his health program so far as, when invited out to dinner, regularly to eat first his own simple supper at home, merely playing with his hostess's food, and taking no chances with lobster and cherries at the same meal.

Both his frugality and his constitutional tendencies conspired to keep him slight, spry and wiry throughout his long life. At the period of which we are now speaking, he was much chagrined at being rejected for military service, both from poor health and undersize, his height being five feet, two inches. Though never athletic, he always walked, four times daily, the short distance, perhaps a quarter mile, between his home and the library.

Traveling, both at home and abroad, was always a favorite relaxation, and from his several voyages to Europe, in 1877, 1902, 1903, 1904 and 1906, he derived much benefit, especially from the actual life on the water. A whimsical, but kindly reference to Mr. Green as an Atlantic voyager may be found in Charles S. Brooks's delightful *Thread of English Road.** Having represented one of the seventeen American libraries at the International London Conference of 1877, he must have been grievously disappointed, in view of his devotion to his profession, love of things English and of ocean travel, to miss the World Conference of 1897, but his name is not among those of the ninety-three Americans in attendance. In 1905, after the A. L. A. Conference at Portland, Oregon, Mr. Green joined the post-conference party of one hundred and fifteen sailing on the "City of Seattle" for Alaska.

Although he received a thorough training for the ministry, as above indicated, and was devoted during all his life to religious, philosophical and historical studies, he never sought or obtained a parish. One sermon, indeed, he did preach in Worcester, but shocked so many straight-grained Puritans by alleging that if Jesus Christ had claimed that two plus two equaled five, there must have been some mistake, that he decided to give up preaching before he really began its practice. It seems probable that three factors conspired to deprive him of a vocation for which he was, in many ways, admirably suited : a fear that his health would not be equal to the brunt

* Pages 75–77.

of parochial routine; an alarming and increasing trouble with his eyesight; and a growing conviction that his over-liberal views on questions of dogmatic theology would fill his position as pastor with embarrassment for himself and his flock.

Always painstaking and accurate in matters of financial detail, the young theologian, probably with many misgivings, accepted, at the age of twenty-seven, the position of bookkeeper in the Mechanics' National Bank of Worcester, and, after a few months, was promoted to the post of teller in the Worcester National Bank, holding this latter position for several years. A further promotion, to the rank of cashier at the Citizens' National Bank, he declined; as also a responsible position in the Worcester County Institution for Savings.

Although January 15, 1871, the date of his first election as librarian, looms up as the great milestone of Mr. Green's career, his official connection with the public library began on New Year's Day of 1867, when he was elected one of the twelve trustees, or directors, as, following the provisions of Dr. Green's will, they are officially designated.

During his term of four years as a director, Mr. Green showed his zeal for his future profession by writing, as secretary of the Library Committee, a report filling twenty-five printed octavo pages, largely on proper methods of cataloging and of circulating books for a public library. Although his approach to his life work must have been tentative and gradual, since, when the president of the board, about 1870, suggested that he stand as a candidate for the post of librarian, he was taken completely by surprise, nevertheless he certainly took up his duties as director with keen relish and enthusiasm and with doubtless a certain feeling of family resentment that his uncle's splendid library was suffering neglect and disuse.

As librarian Mr. Green succeeded Rev. Zephaniah Baker, a Universalist minister, born in Dudley in 1815, and for several years a preacher, till he lost his voice about 1848 and became the Worcester library's first executive in February, 1860. As an avocation he enjoyed fine horses, and showed his versatility by writing and publishing a useful *Cottage Builder's Manual* in 1856, and by compiling the history of his native town of Dudley for Marvin's *Worcester County History* of 1879. According to modern standards, criticism might indeed attach to Mr. Baker for making no determined efforts to get the people of Worcester to use the new "Green Library"; still, the reader should remember that in 1860 the stars of Master Enoch Sneed and Jared Bean were in the ascendant in the library sky, rather than those of such far-seeing prophets as Melvil Dewey and S. S. Green.

Like most stable institutions, the Worcester Public Library spells growth and practical development, rather than arbitrary creation. It was founded, in 1859, by the acceptance, on the part of the city

[24]

council, of Dr. Green's gift of 7500 volumes as the nucleus of the reference library, and of the offer of the "Worcester Lyceum and Library Association" to present their 4350 books to start a circulation department. This latter society, in turn, represented an intellectual partnership of the older "Lyceum," already referred to as founded in 1829, and the "Young Men's Library Association," organized in 1852, and fused with the older society four years later.

Regarding this fortunate consolidation, the kernel of the future public library, the officers of the "Lyceum and Library Association" in their last annual report, for 1860, speak in truly prophetic language:

Although some of our citizens feel that the Public Library is almost an uncalled-for tax upon the community, yet we see by the opening of it, that it was really waited for, and that there were hundreds who stood ready at the first opportunity to show practically how much it was desired. The hundreds who appreciate it will soon become thousands, and the day is not far distant when all our New England cities and many large towns will consider the Public Library as the next necessity to the Public School.

In addition to its own resources, the new-born public library enjoyed, as a neighbor, the library of the Worcester District Medical Society, of some 2400 books, shelved in an adjoining room. Such good neighbors have they proved that never since have they parted company. Worcester's library resources, therefore, in 1860, would exceed 13,000 volumes.

Among many others, less prominent, the names of Edward Everett Hale, Thomas W. Higginson and George F. Hoar may be noted as officers of the "Young Men's Library Association."

On June 18, 1861, the library, which had been open on Foster Street for about a year after its founding, was closed for stock-taking, cataloging, and removal to the new quarters at 18 Elm Street. Owing to delay in furnishing equipment, the Green Library remained closed until early in the following year. This building is still in use for the Circulation, Children's and Medical Departments, housing over 100,000 books in damp basements and hot attics wholly unfitted for the storage of literary property. So substantially was this old brick structure erected that contractors today are quite unwilling to estimate the cost of any structural changes in its walls.

The year 1865 is memorable in the library's annals for the foundation of the reading-rooms. A fund of over $10,000 for their endowment was raised, largely through the enthusiasm of the late Senator Hoar, with Stephen Salisbury, senior, heading the subscription list with a check for $4000. This popular fund unfortunately has suffered some losses by investment, upward of twenty years ago, as its total principal in 1901 was reported at $11,730, and in 1902, $9180, where it has ever since remained.

This is the story of a pioneer who had to blaze his own trails and then lead his public along them, if he could. The first trail that Mr. Green undertook to establish led from the local machine shops to the Green or Reference Library. This comprised an old-fashioned gentleman's library, with such encyclopedias and other reference aids as the times could supply. Listen while Mr. Green tells how he started the trailblazing:

It was thought that the reason why people did not use the library was that they needed assistance in using it. A new librarian was appointed, and allowed to render such aid as was desired by frequenters of the library. Then all persons in the city who had questions to ask, to which they might hope to find answers in books, were cordially invited to come to the library and propound them.

It was made a rule that everybody should be received with courtesy, and made to feel that he is an owner of the library, and that its officers are bound to give a reasonable amount of time to finding answers to his questions. . . . It has been a cardinal principle that the officers should manifest a persistent determination not to allow the inquirer to leave the building without getting — if a possible thing to find it — an answer to his question.

In 1926 the foregoing looks like precepts for the infant class, but in 1871 it was pretty radical doctrine.

After five years of quiet work in Worcester, spent largely in developing a clientèle for the new Green Library, the librarian was ready, at the Centennial Conference of 1876, to deliver his first professional pronouncement: a paper on "Personal Relations between Librarians and Readers." This Philadelphia

Conference, with its registration of 103, was a very business-like and serious gathering. Opening Wednesday, October 4, at 10 a.m., it held three sessions each on that day and the day following, with a seventh (an extra long one) Friday morning and a closing reception the same evening.

Mr. Green's plan was to fix the attention of his hearers by the citation of numerous examples showing how his library had given concrete help to a great variety of persons, and then to deduce some general principles for the guidance of less experienced executives. What impresses the reader most is the astonishingly modern tone of it all, and its homely, downright common sense. The sample questions might come from any reference library today: A wall-painter has a room to ornament; an artisan, the legs of a table to carve; a marble-worker, a lion to engrave in a specified posture; a schoolboy, to show the actual fight between St. George and the dragon; a schoolgirl has heard that the number of feet in a yard-measure was determined by the length of some king's arm. Who was the king?

"There are obvious limits," Mr. Green goes on to say, "to the assistance which a librarian can undertake to render. Common sense will dictate them. Thus, no librarian would take the responsibility of recommending books to give direction for the treatment of disease. Nor would he give legal advice, nor undertake to instruct applicants in regard to the practical manipulations of workshop or laboratory."

Regarding opportunities for service in the Circulation Department Mr. Green says:

Place in the Circulation Department one of the most accomplished of your corps of assistants, some cultivated woman, for example, who heartily enjoys the works of the imagination, but whose taste is educated. She must be a person of pleasant manners, and, while of proper dignity, ready to unbend, and of social disposition. It is well if there is a vein of philanthropy in her composition.

And among his closing aphorisms:

A librarian should be as unwilling to allow an inquirer to leave the library with his question unanswered as a shop-keeper is to have his customer go out of his store without making a purchase. Receive investigators with something of the cordiality displayed by an old-time inn-keeper.

In personal intercourse with readers, there are certain mental tendencies that should be restrained. Idle curiosity is one of them. Many scholars prefer to pursue their studies privately, and are annoyed if they think they are observed.

Respect reticence. If you approach a reader with the purpose of aiding him, and find him unwilling to admit you to his confidence, regard his wishes and allow him to make his investigation by himself.

Be careful not to make inquirers dependent. Give them as much assistance as they need, but try at the same time to teach them to rely upon themselves and become independent.

Avoid scrupulously the propagation of any particular set of views in politics, art, history, philosophy or theology. *Tros Tyriusque mihi nullo discrimine agetur* are words which Virgil puts into the mouth of Queen Dido. The *North American Review* has adopted them for its motto. The promise they contain should be kept by the librarian also. . . . Avoid religiously the practice of cramming the minds of young inquirers with one-sided views regarding questions in dispute.

In conclusion I wish to say that there are few pleasures comparable to that of associating continually with curious and vigorous young minds, and of aiding them in realizing their ideals.

This admirable and prophetic paper created much interest both at Philadelphia and elsewhere. Professor Otis H. Robinson, librarian of Rochester University, said, in commenting on it, at the meeting where it was delivered: "I wish his paper could be read by every librarian and every library director in the country. A librarian should be much more than a keeper of books; he should be an educator."

Of the later interest roused by this paper, Mr. Green himself says in his book of reminiscences, published in 1913:

The description of the work done in Worcester attracted much attention. The Boston *Daily Advertiser* of January 2, 1877 . . . gave an account of the Free Public Library, its features and facilities, and praised warmly the courtesy with which inquirers were received, and the earnest efforts made to secure desired information.

A New York paper took the matter up and improved the occasion, while commending highly the plans in use in Worcester, to speak freely of the unaccommodating spirit which they claimed existed in the large libraries of their own city. The *World* spoke satirically, and after affirming its belief that very few librarians like the one described existed, recommended "that all public librarians and their assistants, besides a knowledge of reading, writing and the four ground rules of arithmetic, be required to pass an examination on this pamphlet, which contains many valuable lessons for the profession."

The *Examiner* of London spoke in a similar spirit, after the close of the International Convention of 1877, in an article (October 13) on the "London Conference of Librarians." Acknowledgment was made of courtesies received in certain large provincial libraries, but the largest in the country, in London, was satirically attacked for lack of courtesy and, by comparison, the spirit shown by Mr. Green in his library was appreciatively described. It was evident then that the great value of libraries as popular educational institutions was not at all generally appreciated.

At about this period of the late seventies and early eighties, modern ideas as to the duties and opportunities of the new American public libraries were beginning to seep down into the public consciousness. In Worcester the first official recommendation on the founding of a public library was made by Hon. Peter C. Bacon, in his inaugural address as mayor, to the city council in 1851. His judgment, however, was far in advance of his associates' in the city government. To the value of the pioneer work by Mr. Green and other enlightened colleagues, testimony in public was given voluntarily by such educators as Charles Francis Adams, at Quincy, and locally by Charles O. Thompson, president, Worcester Polytechnic Institute, Samuel Thurber, principal, Worcester High School, and E. Harlow Russell, principal, Worcester State Normal School.

Said Principal Russell in 1880: "I find, upon inquiry, that, during the current school year, not less than sixty-four per cent of our students have had occasion to visit the Public Library to pursue investigations connected with their studies, several reporting upwards of twenty such visits, and this notwithstanding the fact that the school is situated at a distance from the library, and that we have an excellent, though small, working library of our own."

In 1874 occurred the second of a series of friendly exchanges between Worcester, England, and Worcester, Massachusetts, in which piece of international comity Mr. Green was much interested and highly instrumental. Other occasions of similar import may be found, but these three are cited here because of Mr. Green's enthusiastic participation in everything relating to the mother-city. The first took place in 1846 and was described by Mr. Green in a pamphlet which he wrote in 1908, on the third occasion, to be detailed later. The reader will enjoy a letter printed in this pamphlet, and written by Elihu Burritt, previously referred to as the "Learned Blacksmith":

New Britain, Ct., April 16, '74

Samuel S. Green, Esq.,
My dear Sir: I am very happy to hear that the dear Worcester of my love and pride, where my public life was

born, is going to revive the pleasant communion and fellowship with the old Worcester of Mother England, with which I was somewhat connected nearly thirty years ago.

During the Oregon controversy in 1846, when it was assuming a serious aspect, Joseph Crossfield, a Quaker of Manchester, originated a kind of direct interchange of sentiments on the subject, between English and American towns through friendly international addresses. A great number of these were sent from various towns in England and Scotland to our principal cities. These were all sent to me, or to my care, and I had them printed on slips and posted to several hundred newspapers scattered over the Union. One of these was from Edinburgh to Washington, bearing the names of Dr. Chalmers and the first men of that city. I took this on to Washington myself, and among others showed it to John C. Calhoun, who was deeply interested in it.

At the same time I took with me an address, signed by 1600 ladies of the city of Exeter, England, to the ladies of Philadelphia, who sent a response to it, signed, I believe, by over 3000 of their number. When I went to England in 1846 I took with me this response, and also that of our Worcester to the Mother Worcester in England. Both were presented at public meetings convened for the purpose, and excited the liveliest interest. I have copied out of the *Christian Citizen* for 1846 both communications, which will show you the spirit which they breathed and inspired. . . . I do not know if you have a copy of my last book : *Ten-Minute Talks on All Sorts of Topics* in your library. I have described this friendly international address movement in my autobiography.

Hoping these facts will suffice for your object, I am
                                    Yours truly,
                                              ELIHU BURRITT.

Passing now to the second instance of reciprocity, in 1874, we learn from Mr. Green that, after hearing of a projected visit to England on the part of Hon. John D. Washburn, he, as librarian, proposed to the Board of Directors that the library collect some books relating to the New England Worcester, to be presented to the city council of Worcester, England. The procedure being duly sanctioned by the board, a few books and pamphlets of local interest were collected, specially bound, and delivered to Mr. Washburn. Accompanying the gift was a letter from the board, written by Rev. William R. Huntington, for twenty-one years beloved rector of All Saints Church, and later of Grace Church, New York City:

To the Mayor, Aldermen and Councilors of the City of Worcester, England, the Directors of the Free Public Library in Worcester, in New England, send greeting:
On three several occasions during the past fifty years, once in 1846, and twice since, expressions of kindly feeling have been interchanged between your citizens and our own.

In each of these instances the first word has come from you and the response from us. Encouraged by the memory of these friendly advances, we have thought the present not an unfavorable moment for renewing, by a voluntary act of our own, an acquaintance which we value and should be sorry to see forgotten. . . .

Both cities are centers of a busy agricultural life; both possess manufacturing and commercial industries in singular variety, and both have it for their boast that, notwithstanding the pressure of these material interests, they have not suffered themselves to forget the claims of sound learning and true religion.

May your ancient city prosper and increase. For our own we ask no better fortune than that she may deserve the title that yours has borne so long without dispute : *Civitas in bello et in pace fidelis.*

THOMAS LEVERETT NELSON, *President.*
SAMUEL S. GREEN, *Librarian.*

Worcester, Mass., U. S. A., April 28, 1874.

In acknowledging this courtesy our English brethren closed their letter with this paragraph :

"We confidently trust that the interchange of friendly greetings you have now renewed in so well-timed and graceful a manner may result in a continuing bond of amity between your city and our own, and awaken and keep alive a mutual interest in each other's welfare."

Accompanying this letter were several expensive and beautifully bound books relating to the old Worcester's history.

As Mr. Green always took the keenest delight in furthering mutual comity between the two Worcesters, the reader will learn with interest that the formal opening of the new Worcester (England) Public Library and Hastings Museum, which had been recently founded, was celebrated March 16, 1881. James Russell Lowell, our minister, made the opening speech. Believing that this important occasion should be signalized here in our Worcester, Mr.

[35]

Green requested his directors to assemble in special meeting and to dispatch the following cablegram, which was done forthwith : "The Heart of the Commonwealth greets the ever-faithful city on opening Free library."

So admirably did Mr. Green synchronize this message that the dispatch was put into Mr. Lowell's hand at the moment of his unlocking the new library door, after the procession had reached the building, from the Guildhall.

In his usual happy vein Mr. Lowell remarked, speaking of the respective ages and prospects of the two cities : "I really at my time of life am sometimes doubtful which is best : to have a comfortable past behind you, all settled and arranged, or a future before you, with all its possibilities, it is true, perhaps with all its probabilities, but with some great contingencies also, which sometimes affect the imagination with considerable apprehension!"

In view of Mr. Green's lifelong service to his native city it seems eminently fitting that almost his last official act of importance, which took place within two months of his retirement, should be his participation in the third important exchange of courtesies between the two Worcesters. It was in October, 1908, that Colonel Albert Webb, a distinguished citizen of the old Worcester, informed the mayor of the daughter-city that the writer of the letter had been commissioned by the mayor and corporation to present to the new Worcester two suits of armor reputed to have been worn at the battle of Worcester, in the English civil wars. It happened to be on Guy Fawkes' Day, November 5, that ColonelWebb arrived in Worcester and was welcomed both officially and unofficially in a cordial manner, fully described by Mr. Green in a pamphlet published at the city's expense and entitled: *Worcester, England, and Worcester, Massachusetts.*

For quotation perhaps one paragraph of Colonel Webb's presentation speech will suffice:

We hope that, as a stone thrown into a pool sends its ever-widening ripples toward the banks, be they ever so far distant, this incident will create an ever-broadening movement of cordial good feeling in America toward the mother-country that will be felt even to the farthest confines of the continent. We wish it to be a token and a proof that only the best of good feeling prevails in England toward America, and we hope that the good will which now exists, and is so essential to the peace of the whole world, will be welded into an unbreakable tie between us.

As the name for the settlement at Worcester, Massachusetts, was selected by a committee of Puritans, who had no known connection with the ancient city (always a Royalist stronghold), but since, on the other hand, the *Battle* of Worcester had come to be regarded as God's "crowning mercy" to Cromwell, it appears more than likely that the name was derived from the battle rather than the town. The two suits of armor, therefore, which, by the way, are rather modest and not so very terrifying in appearance, fit quite aptly into this derivation. For several years they decorated the public library art rooms, rousing much curiosity on the part of school-children and other visitors of inquisitive temper. About five years ago, however, a mandate came from City Hall that they should be promoted to a peg of fame in the municipal building, so that now when you pass its massive portals, if you will gaze heavenward toward the zenith of that blue-white archway, toward the rear of the main corridor, you may behold them hanging meekly on their hooks, and looking forward confidently to the early completion of their tercentenary of "innocuous desuetude."

The last scene of these excellent exchanges was staged in June, 1921, when Dr. Albert E. Cross, with a party of Rotarians en route for the international conference at Edinburgh, stopped at Worcester to present a bronze tablet now adorning a wall of the Guildhall of the ancient city. The center of the tablet represents the new Worcester's City Hall, flanked on either side by smoke-belching factories, typifying the character of the city. Two shields approximate the British and American flags respectively, with the city's seal between them. Under a pair of crossed olive branches at the center is the legend : "Presented to the city of Worcester, England, by the city of

Worcester, Massachusetts, June 6, 1921," and in an oval border, enclosing the whole : "Worcester, Massachusetts, a city of opportunity and diversified industries."

In our national life, the decade of the eighties was devoted largely to expansion and internal development, with ample opportunity for selfish individuals and corporations to lay up money, unhampered by governmental control. Our library conscience, however, easily outran that of the business world, so that, while our plutocrats were digging their foundations wide and deep, with no such bugaboo as the "Sherman Act" yet heard of, our A. L. A. was growing each year a sturdier child, and by the end of the decade had become a recognized educational force.

From the beginning of the "accelerated library movement" in 1876 up to 1893, Mr. Green had been continuously active in national library affairs. During nearly the whole time he had been one of the inner circle of officers who guided the movements of the A. L. A. and in constant and immediate association with the leading spirits who not only animated the action of the organization, but were especially earnest and effective in bringing about library development in general. He had attended all the conferences of the A. L. A., served on committees, made numerous reports, presented many papers, and joined constantly in discussions. He had been a regular contributor to the *Library Journal*, had actively engaged in local library movements, and done everything in his power to advance the library cause.

In addition to the generous amount of time which Mr. Green gave to the upbuilding of the American public library, his efforts at home were largely devoted to the extension of the work with schools; the further popularizing of the Green or Reference Library, and the campaign for a new library building to supplement the structure of 1861. So successful were his efforts and those of his Board of Directors in this latter affair, that before the close of 1888 the city had bought the adjacent lot east on Elm Street, comprising about nine thousand square feet, for $35,000, and on April 1, 1891, the structure which in 1926 is euphemistically termed the "New Building" was enthusiastically opened to the public.

On this momentous occasion the most striking feature was (for Worcester) a monster loan-exhibition of no less than 129 oil paintings of Worcester citizens, past and present. Salisburys, Lincolns, Davises, Rices, Greens and scores of representatives of other prominent families, who had submitted to the gentle accolade of the artist's brush, rubbed elbows in that goodly company. Thanks might be well rendered to the Worcester Art Society for its prodigious activity in assembling a galaxy like this.

Incidentally it may be remarked, among Mr. Green's activities, that for many years before the founding of the excellent local Art Museum in 1898, the public library used its best efforts to take on the functions of an art museum in addition to its own. Among Mr. Green's best friends in forwarding the city's art interests was his pastor, Rev. Austin S. Garver, a true art lover and connoisseur, whose dignified and sympathetic appreciation of Mr. Green's life work in Worcester may be read in the *Library Journal* for June, 1909.

One form of bibliographical activity from which this twentieth century enjoys a blessed immunity is the issue of the complete (?) printed library catalog. In the seventies and eighties this mania was truly pestilential, and Mr. Green a proud and willing sufferer from a disease which proved practically endemic even among the most accomplished members of the profession. Printed catalogs like those of the Astor, Peabody or Boston Athenaeum are, of course, permanent monuments of bibliographical and historical value; the uncomplimentary references here made relate to the attempts of all libraries that could afford it, to print the so-called complete catalogs of their circulation departments, for home use.

Catalogs of the Worcester Public Library have been printed as follows: in 1861 a modest volume of 186 pages, with equally humble *Addenda*, half the size, in 1867. Three years later the whole was revised and issued as *Catalogue of the Circulating Department*, to which a supplement was added, 1874. Ten years later appeared Mr. Green's truly *magnum opus* of 1392 pages, under the title: *Catalogue of the Circulating and Part of the Intermediate (Reference) Department*, followed by supplements in 1889 and 1896.

In making his happy announcement of the appearance of this prodigious undertaking, Mr. Green states that an edition of 3000 copies has been ordered, and that "its cost, aside from the labor involved in its preparation for the press and in proof-reading, has been thus far $3533.73. $900 additional will be required for binding. It is proposed to sell the work at seventy-five cents a copy, that is to say for about one half the cost of paper, printing and binding."

In his pioneer work on the relations of libraries and schools, Mr. Green read a paper on this subject before the American Social Science Association at its Saratoga meeting in September, 1880 (printed in the *Library Journal* for October). Employing his favorite method of practical illustration, he tells how, late in the autumn of 1879, four educators met to consider the future possibilities of their work: the superintendent of schools, a member of the school committee, the principal of the local normal school, and the city librarian. They agreed at once that studies in the three upper grades (for example) would be made pleasanter and more profitable if increased school and library cooperation could be secured.

The first concrete attempt was to choose the subject of geography, to be illustrated, in school work, by attractive books from the library. Mr. Green was invited by the superintendent to try his plan before the grade teachers at an early date.

The teachers listened in an interested manner, and many of them showed not only readiness but anxiety to undertake the work suggested. The Librarian then invited them to select some country that they would like to have illustrated by means of books belonging to the library. They selected one, and came to the library, the next half-holiday, to listen to the promised exposition. The Librarian had before him, say, one hundred volumes relating to the country in the description of which aid was to be afforded, and pointed out wherein the value of each one consisted to assist teachers and scholars in studying geography. They saw at once valuable aid could be had from the library in their work of teaching, and the next step taken by the Librarian was to invite them to tell him what countries the children were studying about at that time, and to keep him informed in regard to those they were at work upon at other times, in order that he might help them to pick out works suitable for school use.

In this same paper Mr. Green quotes Samuel Thurber, principal of the local high school:

There is a post-meridian session of the school every day over in Elm Street. While the regular teachers are hurrying and worrying with their college classes, these afternoon teachers in the other building are patiently having their session which ends at no particular time, but only when each questioner is answered. We do not see why these Elm Street folks are not just as much high school teachers as those who congregate each morning in the great building with the tower. . . . As an ally of the high school the public library is not merely useful, it is absolutely indispensable.

Again, Mr. Green touches, before the close of this paper, another vital matter, of equal importance to-day:

Sufficient care is not taken to designate the age of children for whom particular books are designed. What is wanted specially is a selection of books for children between the ages of eleven and fifteen, every one of which is known from perusal by competent persons to be a really good book, and one adapted to the capacity of young folks.

The advocacy of the use of the telephone for library purposes seems, in 1880, a suggestion well ahead of the times.

If the decade of the eighties was the period of careful and tender planting, watering and cultivating the library field on the part of Mr. Green and his pioneer colleagues, the early nineties showed the harvest ripe for the sickle. First came the creation, in October, 1890, of the Massachusetts Free Public Library Commission, with C. B. Tillinghast, librarian of the State Library, as chairman. At that time 103 of the 351 towns or cities of the commonwealth had no free library facilities. Largely as a result of the Commission's efforts, this number was gradually lessened, and by 1904 was reduced to zero. Of the five original members of this Commission, the first to be established in the United States, Miss Elizabeth P. Sohier, of Beverly, is still serving; Mr. Green, also a "charter member," was Mr. Tillinghast's right hand man, and the obvious expert on all matters relating to public library administration. He served continuously for nineteen years until he resigned all official work in 1909.

Much activity was shown by this Commission, its first report, for 1891, forming a substantial volume of 290 pages, the bulk of which comprised a handbook of Massachusetts libraries, with complete data on history, administration, finance, trustees past and present, etc., with many illustrations of library buildings. The later handbook of 1899, revised and extended, comprises 465 well-illustrated pages and has always since that date been more or less of a "collector's item" for library school students.

The year 1891 offered a double satisfaction to Mr. Green, bringing to fruition his dreams of a new library building, and conferring on him the highest honor in the gift of his colleagues, the presidency of the A. L. A. Both Mr. Green and Mr. Frank P. Hill, the secretary, were emergency officers and had to work hard to prepare a program on short notice for the annual conference, which was held that year in San Francisco. They were successful, however, and the eighty delegates present, forty of whom were from the east, were enthusiastic in their praises of the conference. The presidential address dwelt on the duty of a library to its community and described the methods which had been adopted since 1876 for making American public

libraries the most efficient in the world. Its first two
sentences fairly state his professional platform in the
tersest of homely phrase: "The function of a library
is to serve its users. It is the duty of a public library
to serve the public."

Mr. Green had good reason for the belief which he
expressed that this conference of 1891 planted much
of that fertile seed which has sprung up and made
California a leader in library work, and made possible
an attendance of 582 at the next conference to be held
there just twenty years later.

In spite of the general enthusiasm shown at the
conference, the President found the hospitalities extended to the delegates somewhat over-profuse. In
fact "the conviction became strong that so much entertainment during the period of sessions made the
members somewhat languid or otherwise unfitted
them for work, and that some of the future conferences should be held in quiet places, free from the se-
ductions of large and generous cities."

Among the projects of the San Francisco meeting of
1891 was the plan for an exhibition of library work, in
connection with the World's Fair of 1893, including
the preparation of the original *Catalog of "A. L. A."
Library*, 5000 volumes. With Melvil Dewey, Frederick
M. Crunden and Miss M. S. R. James (librarian of
the People's Palace, London), Mr. Green shared the
honor of presiding for a day over the International
Congress of Librarians.

This international feature of the 1893 conference, Mr. Green says, was not specially pronounced, as 200 of the participants were Americans, the foreign contingent comprising two men and two women from England, one German and one Canadian. Some foreigners sent papers, however, to be read.

Twenty addresses, six by foreigners, were scheduled for delivery and all but three presented. Some tendencies of German librarianship may be inferred from the title of a paper by Dr. O. Hartwig of the University of Halle: "On the Direct Loan of MSS. from one Library to Another, and on the Foundation of a Society for the Phototypic Multiplication of Important MSS. not Subject to Direct Loan." Mr. Green's paper was on the then new topic of state library commissions.

In his book of library reminiscences Mr. Green recalls that during the progress of the meeting over which he presided, Mr. R. R. Bowker introduced to the audience Sir Walter Besant, who had presided at a meeting in another division of the Department of Literature. It was his novel *All Sorts and Conditions of Men* which prompted the establishment of the People's Palace, London, whose librarian, Miss James, was mentioned as being present at this conference, and presiding on the last day.

Regarding his connection with national library affairs, Mr. Green considers 1893 a proper date for bringing his professional memories to a close. "After 1893 although I attended many conventions, wrote a number of papers, and took a general interest in the library movement, I gradually ceased to keep in touch with the details of new propositions; relaxed somewhat intimacy with other librarians, and failed to keep conversant with the inside knowledge of the workings of leaders which I had hitherto enjoyed." But in Worcester his work, as measured by years of usefulness, was not much more than half completed.

CHAPTER III

TOWARD the close of the nineties, Mr. Green pushed, with his customary vigor, the reorganization of the Circulation Department, and consequent revision of the card catalog. In 1891, on entering the new building, he introduced the Decimal Classification for the Reference and Green Libraries, but continued the use of the old "accession order" for several years longer, in the Circulation Department. About 1895, however, some extra money was extracted from the city; catalogers from Albany were engaged, and the hoary fastnesses of the feudal system attacked with a will. From this time on the patrons of home reading could "rummage" (to use Mr. Green's favorite word) among the shelves with some real satisfaction. Can an ambitious librarian visualize a more dismal condition than to have to work in an unclassified library?

From 1895 dates the earliest beginning of Worcester's present branch library system. Quoting from Mr. Green's report for that year:

Last spring a delivery station was established at Greendale (a suburb some four miles from City Hall). This has been conducted at the expense of the residents of that suburb. The cost is very small.

An expressman going through Greendale on his way from West Boylston to Worcester stops at a store in Greendale every Wednesday and Saturday; takes thence a locked box of books, and cards of users, to the library building, and calling at the latter place in the afternoon, takes the box, filled with newly selected books back to the store, at which residents call for them.

The eight delivery stations which operated during the palmy days of this service have, in all but two instances, given way to branch library service.

The end of this decade, of the nineties, found Mr. Green nearly sixty-four years old and in excellent physical condition. Although practically at the age when the federal government calls for the resignations of its employees, it is doubtful if any thought of relinquishing his post ever occurred to him at this period, or for some time to come.

The year 1900 saw the completion of a minor addition to the old building and the opening of the Children's Department. Says the librarian, of this latter much needed innovation : "The Children's Room has been a great success. There has been a rush of children wishing to have cards and take out books. Between the hours of 4.15 and 5.45 o'clock in the afternoon, accommodations are taxed to the utmost."

Of some of his pioneer work Mr. Green says, about the time of his completion of twenty-five years' service : "This library was the first of any in the large towns in New England to open its doors on Sunday (December 8, 1872) for purposes of reference and reading. That plan long ceased to be an experiment, and from the beginning has given satisfaction to the users of the library and the serious portion of the community. Our example was followed immediately by the Public Library of Boston, and the plan has been very generally adopted throughout the country."

Among the archives of the Worcester Public Library is a document of forty-four pages, dated May 4, 1904, in Mr. Green's characteristic handwriting, the opening portion of which will interest the reader, as it contains the first inkling of his retirement from active service, which was not to take place till about five years later.

To a committee of five members (of the Board of Library Directors) which is considering more minutely than usually the present condition of this library,

GENTLEMEN : Considering the uncertainty of some members of the City Government regarding the prevalence of economy in the management of this library, and the necessary unfamiliarity of most of the members of the Board of Directors with the details of library work, I agreed heartily with you in respect to the advisability of having the library examined by an expert, who was likely to make a disinterested report regarding the management of the institution, I can endorse heartily several of his recommendations, and am impressed by his just and kindly spirit.

The expert in question was Melvil Dewey, then director of the New York State Library, who had been invited by the directors, some time before, to make a general survey of the library, and report with special reference to the possibility of improving the service. Although this act of the board might not necessarily be regarded as an indication of hostility toward Mr. Green or of dissatisfaction with his administration, it may as well be stated now that, about this time, there appeared on the library board a very active element, determined to bring about his early retirement. This element never secured an actual majority in the board, but approached it closely, and more than made up, in cohesive persistency, what it lacked in actual numbers. In defense of this attitude of certain members of the board, it should in fairness be stated that, in spite of Mr. Green's devoted zeal in popularizing his library, a number of honest patrons of the institution, who did not establish personal contact with the librarian, found the library atmosphere sometimes a little chilly.

This condition of affairs naturally clouded and saddened the last six or seven years of Mr. Green's incumbency, and was particularly galling in the case of one who justly felt himself an expert in his own field, and who for over thirty years had been considered an undisputed authority, at least before his Board of Directors, on all matters relating to library work. Even with this handicap he retained his position till well toward the end of his seventy-second year.

If Mr. Green could not escape the feeling that Mr. Dewey's visit to Worcester and subsequent report were instigated through no kindly regard for his administration, he must have felt gratified on reading the following extracts from the Committee's report:

It must be a matter of gratification to us all that this gentleman [Mr. Dewey] of acknowledged reputation among librarians, and well competent to judge of the condition of our library, should make so favorable and complimentary a report, and the citizens of Worcester should, and doubtless will, exhibit a new pride in their Public Library, when they read the well-deserved tribute to its accomplishments in the past, its leadership and its condition today. They may be justly proud of the results of the liberal policy that, from the first inception of the library, has characterized its administration, its relation to the public and to the educational departments of our city.

Some of Mr. Dewey's comments or suggestions have rather wide application, such as that the word "free" should be stricken from the library's official title. It is commonly understood that in technical library parlance "free" means "open for the general use of all comers" and that "public" means "wholly or largely supported by taxation," and therefore, in any ordinary human contingency, here in these United States, the term "public" would certainly include the idea contained in "free." It is true that Mr. Green himself, in commenting on this suggestion, tells us that the members of the Massachusetts Library Commission retained the word "free" in addition to "public" because public libraries were not always free. The only instance that he cites, however, is Springfield, where the right to use the library was not always universal. As the Springfield library, however, includes neither of the two words in question in its official title but is called the "City Library Association," its name can hardly be adduced to support Mr. Green's argument. As the Worcester library had been incorporated, under Dr. Green's will, with the longer name, using also the term "director" instead of the more usual "trustee" for the same reason, it seemed inexpedient to act on these two minor recommendations.

With the term "Intermediate library" the case appeared different to the directors, who followed Mr. Dewey's suggestion that the phrase be discontinued. It had been devised by Mr. Green to signify reference books not in the Green library, or books of a reference character but not bought from the Green funds, and therefore not subject to the provision that they should be used only in the library buildings.

As the Worcester library is shelved in perhaps a unique manner, it may interest the reader to give this point a moment's attention. The quarter of a million books comprising the whole library are divided roughly in halves, and shelved separately : the Circulation and Children's Department in the old building, with the Reference and Green Libraries in the other. This plan aims to remove from circulation, by keeping the cards out of the circulation catalog, that large collection, found in any good sized library, of books obsolete, bulky, rare or otherwise unsuitable for home use, but for which inexperienced persons would often apply on their call-slips, only to be disappointed, in many instances, with the results of their researches in the card catalog. The chief difficulty at Worcester is that call-numbers are often identical in the two departments, except for certain arbitrary distinguishing symbols, and if these are omitted by patrons of the Reference Department, the pages have to guess (on very flimsy evidence) in which department to look. The reference card-catalog is complete, of course, for the whole system.

On the question of an assistant-librarian the Special Committee, following Mr. Dewey, reported: "The librarian is as active and interested today as he has ever been, but he unites in the opinion of the Committee that the time has arrived when, in order to accomplish the best results, it is advisable that he have a male assistant who can relieve him of various details of the work, and assume some portion of the responsibility of administration, while materially assisting in the contemplated extension of library work and usefulness."

Mr. Green's last annual report expresses the opinion that an assistant librarian should be a woman, his reasons being that two of the assistant's chief duties are library housekeeping and a close and intimate touch with woman department-heads.

Mr. Green's primary professional interests centered undoubtedly around the development of his beloved Reference Library. All his reports abound with enthusiastic accounts of the benefits conferred upon the city by the presence of this admirable representative of the "people's university." In the arranging of exhibitions, both of material owned by the library and lent from outside, he was uncommonly resourceful. In his annual report for 1905 he describes, in addition to the exhibition of the processes of bookbinding, lent by the Newark library, and supplemented by local resources, one relating to work with the blind : "A number of books were selected from our collection (of books for the blind) printed in various types, and representatives of the blind came, some one day and some another, to show the public how they read the books. They also brought slates for writing. . . . This exhibition excited wide interest in the community. The blind were gratified by it, as it awakened a lively interest in their plans for getting a living, and for improvement in attainments."

Unabated energy and mental vigor characterized the closing as well as all other years of Mr. Green's administration. In his very last report, for 1908, he points out the imperative need of five branch libraries and tells of his conference with the city engineer as to their proper positions.

Likewise in the same report : "I have long felt it desirable to do something which, in so far as I can learn from correspondence, has not yet been done elsewhere, namely, provide a large room well stocked with books, and with a pleasant attendant, for young persons, too old to use the children's room, and yet too young to use the general library without sympathetic aid."

CHAPTER IV
EVENING — AFTERGLOW

IN presenting his letter of resignation on January 12, 1909, after thirty-eight valiant years of unbroken service, Mr. Green requested also the reading of an earlier letter, written five years previous, which will interest the reader:

Worcester, January 6, 1904.

To Hon. Alfred S. Pinkerton,
President Board of Directors,

MY DEAR MR. PINKERTON: Will you please present my resignation as Librarian to the Board of Directors? If a sudden withdrawal would be embarrassing to the Board, I shall be happy to give sympathetic consideration to its wishes.

Very truly yours,
SAMUEL SWETT GREEN.

Being told by the President and another member of the Board, whose opinion I especially valued, that it was likely that the interests of the library would suffer greatly if I were to resign at that time, I withdrew the letter before it had been presented to the Board. This action was taken very reluctantly. Every year since 1904 I have wished earnestly to resign, but have not felt at liberty to do so until today.

While I have been a librarian, I have been a student also. Many years ago I determined to put into suitable form some of the results of my experience, thought and research, and have laid out work which it will take several years to perform. This should be begun at once, for, though

[58]

vigorous in mind and body, I cannot permanently count, at the age of nearly seventy-two years, upon a long continuation of vitality. If the work which I am undertaking is important, and it seems to me to be so, I must begin it and work industriously before my body fails to serve me, and the faculties of my mind decay. A year or two must be spent in quietly reviewing the works which have been most influential in the formation of my opinions, before putting my thoughts into the literary form which I have in mind.

This explanation will make it evident that I cannot properly remain longer [dated January 12, 1909] in my present position. I have not yet reached the age of reminiscence, but still live in the future. The future, however, is necessarily uncertain. My change of occupation must begin at once, and the announcement of withdrawal from the place of Librarian be regarded as final and irrevocable.

An obvious reference may be inferred above to a literary work of different character from Mr. Green's *Public Library Movement* published in 1913. This was never put into type, but was completed as an extended essay, comprising four or five chapters and entitled, significantly, *Peace in Doubt*. This illuminating title offers quite a definite suggestion as to why the author never sought a parochial charge.

And so on January 12, 1909, a terribly inclement, stormy and slippery day, Mr. Green's phenomenal term of thirty-eight years of continuous service to his native city came to an end. Such an event could not pass unnoticed in Worcester's official family, and largely through the influence of Mayor James Logan, a splendid Scotch-American of the Carnegie type, with a vast respect for the printed page, the farewell dinner to Mr. Green at the Worcester Club on March 11, assembled forty-six of the city's best-known residents. Among them were Mr. Justice Arthur P. Rugg, now Chief Justice, Massachusetts Supreme Court, Mayor James Logan and three ex-mayors, Edward J. McMahon, Esq., president of the Board (gracious and accomplished toastmaster of the evening), together with many of the city's leading business and professional men.

Referring to the twenty-four toasts, quoted by Mr. McMahon as having been drunk at Worcester's first recorded civic banquet, when independence was announced here, July 14, 1776, Mayor Logan began with an apology for "talking shop," saying that he wished to make some references to the paper industry, with which, as an envelope manufacturer, he had enjoyed lifelong familiarity.

Speaking first of the shaking of the vat, in the hand-paper industry (reminding one of Eden Phillpotts's admirable story of English handicraft, *Storm in a Teacup*), Mr. Logan went on to tell how paper-making appears, in a sense, as a "barometer to register the education, the knowledge, the accumulated wisdom, the intelligence of the civilized world."

Quoting Dr. Van Dyke's *School of Life* Mr. Logan continued: "Through books we become acquainted with those men who by faith saw the invisible, and brought it within our range of vision, for we need to remember that it is not the eye, but the mind which most truly sees. Through the mind, the inventor, with the eye of faith, saw the machine before pencil had been put upon paper, and, his faith laying hold upon the thing hoped for, saw his device, which was to lighten human toil, and bring the comforts of life within the reach of millions, become a reality."

"We have met tonight," said the Mayor in closing, "to give expression to our appreciation of the work of this faithful public servant, who, through his larger knowledge of books, has introduced so many of us into his wider circle of the great men of the earth, the record of whose life work is and will continue to be, an inspiration to the youth of coming times. Without the aid of the library most of these men would be strangers to us, and we should not even be conscious of our debt of obligation to them. By the aid of the books and the library and the librarian, they are our intimate friends and personal acquaintances, many of whom have been introduced to us by our honored guest, with whom we meet tonight, and our lives are richer by the wider circle of acquaintance into which we have entered by his aid."

In addition to the Mayor's address and the witty introductions and punctuations of the toastmaster, the printed menu (which was embellished by Mr. Green's photograph) called for speeches "For Past Directors" by Judge William T. Forbes; "For Present Directors" by Professor Zelotes W. Coombs and some remarks by the librarian, closing with Mr. Green's response.

After making due acknowledgments of the great honor paid to him, Mr. Green went on to say :

I have always wished to be counted among the men of toil. My enjoyment has been found mainly in work . . . in regard to my age I may say that my vigor is such that I should today be the unhappiest man in Worcester, if not allowed to do every day a hard day's work.

I do not care to rest, but desire time and a sense of freedom that will enable me pleasantly to continue my studies and, if it seems advisable, to write out some of the results of investigation, thought and experience.

When Charles H. Morgan, who, I am sorry to hear, is kept away from this meeting by infirmity, came upon the Board of Directors of the Free Public Library, I remember that I conceived for him at once a great admiration. Here was a man who was doing effective work to lay here the foundations of that material prosperity which must exist before educational institutions can be built, including a good public library.

I have always had a great admiration for men who can do something; who can do the work that I am engaged in better than I can, and can do other kinds of work that I cannot possibly do. I have always had a low opinion of my abilities; it may surprise some of you to learn this. I do not know how I could have accomplished what I have done, had it not been that I have contempt for men who are shams, and at the same time conceitedly ignorant or unworthily vain. . . .

When Henry Willis, a former Mayor of Worcester, England, came to our Worcester for a day, his entertainment was placed in the hands of the President of the Library Board and myself, the Librarian. Among other things done for him, a reception was prepared at the library in the rooms then occupied by the Worcester District Medical Society. The guests had assembled, and while waiting for Mr. Willis, were conversing easily. Our dear friend, the late Senator Hoar, raising his eyes saw nearby a glass case which held the bones of a human skull. Turning to the late Judge Aldrich, he said: "Do you know that these bones, when put together, make the skull of an earlier librarian who was worn out by his efforts to get from the City Government money enough to carry on the work of the library properly?"

There is another side to the matter, however. I once had the pleasure of listening to our distinguished townswoman, Mrs. Daniel Merriam, as she gave a lecture on portrait painting. She sat in a handsome chair, clad in a gown made perhaps by Worth of Paris, at any rate worthy to have been made by that famous artist. With a little table before her supporting her manuscript, she daintily turned the leaves, and, herself a beautiful picture, described portrait painting to us. She said in her essay that, when seated at the table on Thanksgiving Day, in the midst of a happy company, she had sometimes wished that somebody would write a paper from the standpoint of the turkey. Making an application of her remarks she said that she would like to have a paper written from the point of view of the sitter or stander, the victim in portrait painting.

Gentlemen, I cannot look at you without feelings of contrition. The pressure brought to bear on you to give us money to supply the reasonable wants of the library was tremendous. As we fired at you a long series of unanswerable arguments which you knew you must make a show of controverting, your health must have suffered in consequence.

Some of your members have died. I must believe, however, in the doctrine of the survival of the fittest. My explanation is that mayors who have died did not yield quickly enough. The strain became so great as to impair their constitution, and plant in them the seeds of disease which led to their early death.

General Sprague had had the wisdom to marry one of my assistants. She had made him acquainted with the needs of the library. He yielded to our appeals summarily. You see what happened. He is now as vigorous as a young man, at the age of eighty-two. For the life of me I cannot understand why he is not here with the other boys tonight. . . .

One of the highest compliments paid to Mr. Green on this momentous occasion was an impromptu address by Justice Arthur P. Rugg, who said, with a true touch of prophecy: "The people of Worcester don't appreciate the distinction that Librarian Green has given us. The history of libraries will never be written without the name of Samuel S. Green written large."

As a substantial token of their esteem, his fellow citizens assembled around the tables, presented to the guest of honor two volumes of Pennell's *Life of Whistler*, sumptuously bound for the occasion, together with a bouquet of forty-two roses, symbolic of his lifelong service to the city: thirty-eight as librarian and four as a member of the Board of Directors.

Mr. Green's last opportunity to appear in public as

a representative of the institution to whose advancement he had devoted practically all his life, occurred before the end of that same year, 1909, a year memorable as the date of his retirement, and also as the fiftieth anniversary of the founding of the library, on December 23. To have made a Christmas present to the people of Worcester was an act of generous and substantial beneficence on the part of Dr. Green, but if he had offered his gift a month earlier or later, the fiftieth anniversary would have doubtless attracted more popular attention. Being held, as a true anniversary, on the night before Christmas Eve, with everybody busy with Yuletide activities, the jubilee brought out only a small audience of less than one hundred persons.

In addition to the speakers of March 11 (the mayor, the president of the board, Mr. Green and the librarian) the heads of the four Worcester colleges spoke or sent greetings: Rev. Thomas E. Murphy for Holy Cross College; Dr. Francis R. Lane for the Normal School; Dr. Edmund A. Engler for the local Polytechnic; and Dr. G. Stanley Hall for Clark University.

A paragraph from Mayor Logan is well worth quoting: "In the Latin tongue the word for 'book' and the word for 'free' is the same, namely, *liber*. That may be simply an etymological coincidence, but it may be taken, nevertheless, to indicate a profound truth. Through the free library, books will free men's minds from the shackles of ignorance, and, what is quite as important, they will also free the mind from bondage to outworn ideals and wrong conceptions of life, and of man's relation to the great universe in which we live."

Mr. Green's address on this occasion naturally took the form of a survey of his professional achievements since 1871, together with a forecast of immediate needs in the future. Most of the historical points have been already covered in this essay, with the exception of the three following:

About the year 1870 a great and sudden interest in art sprang up in Massachusetts. It was widespread. Villages took on a new appearance, owing to the care which was taken of grounds, and of the attempt at taste in building and painting houses. Interior decorations began to multiply. This movement showed itself, however, particularly in cities. It became evident to me that this new interest should be immediately attended to. . . . Having found that it would be proper for us to use the income of the Green Library Fund to buy photographs, we began to purchase from the old and the new masters in painting, sculpture and architecture, of large size, to gratify the awakened interest of older persons. We continued also the close alliance with the Art Society, furnishing that institution with lighted and heated art galleries, it paying all other expenses of not infrequent exhibitions of oil paintings.

The excellence of our methods has found recognition in France and Germany. A communication was made through the State Department at Washington to a former Mayor, stating that changes were to be made in the libraries of the

Seine, and asking for information regarding the conduct of this institution. The compliment was the greater, as only a very small number of libraries was questioned regarding their management. Notice was taken of the material itself in a printed report of the Department subsequently published.

Constantin Nörrenberg, an officer in the University of Schleswig-Holstein, on his way home after the Chicago Exposition of 1893, visited this library and showed great interest in the manner in which work is done here. On going back to Germany he wrote a book in which he advocated the introduction into that country of popular libraries such as we have in the United States, and described this institution as a model worthy of imitation.

With characteristic energy and foresight Mr. Green proceeds a little later : "So much for the work which has been done here. I cannot be content, however, to speak of the past only. My thoughts turn almost exclusively to the future. There is a large number of improvements which I should like to see made in this institution, but their introduction here depends largely on increased accommodations and expenditures."

Of the two pressing needs which Mr. Green outlines, that for branch libraries he lived to see realized in 1914, but the new main building is not yet.

Fitting notice of Mr. Green's retirement was taken officially by the Board of Directors in giving him the title of Librarian Emeritus; a quiet office for his exclusive use; and the service of his competent and favorite secretary for an hour daily, whenever needed. The habits of nearly forty years in coming daily to the library, made these privileges not only welcome but almost indispensable.

The two literary efforts mentioned previously occupied most of Mr. Green's working hours, in retirement. On their completion in 1913, he had finished his seventy-sixth year, after which his health failed gradually till he finally succumbed at the Maple Hall Sanitarium, on Sunday evening, December 8, 1918, when well advanced in his eighty-second year. Although very feeble toward the end, he insisted, with characteristic pertinacity, on maintaining his wonted schedule of spending his mornings at the library, to the utmost limit, and did so (latterly by the use of a taxicab) till November 27, which was practically also the date of his entering the sanitarium.

Funeral services were not held in Worcester, but were conducted privately by an old friend, the Rev. Charles Fletcher Dole, of Jamaica Plain, at the Forest Hills Crematory Chapel. The quiet dignity of this service, attended only by a few whom Mr. Green had known best, formed a fitting close to a life spent modestly with the single aim of bringing satisfaction and happiness into the lives of his fellow men. His lasting monument will be the Worcester Public Library, to which his uncle has indeed given the name and the endowment, while it was the nephew who vitalized it with the breath of life.

To characterize Mr. Green socially is not easy, as he combined elements of reserve and of camaraderie in an unusual manner. An old friend and companion, Dr. Charles L. Nichols, a ripe scholar and generous citizen, has given the following personal recollections :

My personal memories of Mr. Green are so rich that it is a pleasure to add my word of commendation to what is already written.

We were members of several societies — social and literary — where we frequently met, two of which in particular can be mentioned.

As a member of the St. Wulstan Society, Mr. Green showed a mind ripe for the discussion of every topic brought forward and his particular concern — The Roman remains in England — was a source of constant interest at our gatherings because he kept in touch with the most recent progress by frequent visits to that country.

As a member of the Council of the American Antiquarian Society, he was always present at its meetings, and was ready to give sound advice on its problems and to bear his share of its burdens.

My earliest recollection of Mr. Green was in his capacity of Librarian of our Public Library. In those years my interest in the progress of physical science brought me many problems and to all my questions he gave me satisfactory answers.

If our library did not possess the most recent books on these subjects he turned to the Boston Public Library, which purchased the books, if not already on its shelves, and sent them to Worcester, for our use, in accordance with the generous policy of that great institution.

Mr. Green was a rare man — an idealist on the one hand, and on the other unusually practical in his efforts to bring a knowledge of books and their contents to the minds of the young, not merely of Worcester but the whole country.

The St. Wulstan Society is named from the famous Saxon bishop who held the see of Worcester at the time of the Norman Conquest; this little club comprises sixteen of the city's cleverest talkers.

Another familiar acquaintance and professional colleague during forty years, the veteran William E. Foster of Providence, writes thus from his heart:

It has been a fortunate thing, in the development of American libraries, that its leaders have represented various types, and have had various antecedents. Some of them, as we know, have come to their work after systematic training in library schools, while others have owed the keen interest which led them to undertake the work, to their previous service on a board of library trustees. Justin Winsor was a conspicuous instance of the latter type; and to this type also belonged Mr. Green.

The fact that the needs of the library had appealed to him as a trustee had the effect of greatly facilitating the recognition, in the community, of the claims of the local library's work. But Mr. Green, from the start, was intimately concerned in the general diffusion of interest in libraries throughout the country. It was this which led him to welcome heartily the measures which led to the formation of the American Library Association, and of the various local organizations.

In Mr. Green's contact with others, both in the case of the readers using his own library, and of those engaged in library work elsewhere, personality played an important part. A cheerful outlook on life, a cordial greeting, a helpful attitude,— these were the factors in his personality which made him successful as a librarian, and which render his memory a delightful one on which to look back.

Dr. Louis N. Wilson, versatile and successful university librarian for thirty-five years, writes of Mr. Green's connection with the early days of Clark University:

When I was appointed Librarian at Clark, in the spring of 1889, our Founder impressed upon me the fact that Worcester had one of the best equipped Public Libraries in the country and he advised me to see Mr. Samuel S. Green who would gladly co-operate with us in building up our Library at the University. During those early years of our history I saw a great deal of Mr. Green. He suggested that our professors and students use the Public Library freely and thus avoid duplication so far as possible. As our funds at that time were limited he ordered a large number of sets of scientific journals and many books of reference for our use. He also gave me a great deal of advice which I sadly needed as a novice in library work.

Mr. Green was a good book-buyer and constantly enriched the Worcester collection so that today it is remarkably well equipped along reference lines. He was, perhaps, over anxious about the use of books, but not more so than were his contemporaries in the same field. He was one who delighted to run down a reference and would take no end of time and pains in doing so, but his idea of a library was that the great majority should come and use the books only in the building. To his intimate friends, however, he was most liberal, both in buying for them and in allowing them to take books from the library.

SAMUEL SWETT GREEN

Judged by the standards of today Mr. Green was very conservative, yet he was far in advance of the average librarian of his early days. It was hard for him to understand the new library spirit that John Cotton Dana brought to Springfield in 1898, and he had serious misgivings as to its wisdom. He was very impatient of criticism, yet he took it and profited by it.

I think Mr. Green is entitled to a place among the early American librarians — men like Poole, Fletcher, Billings and others — who prepared the way for the wonderful later development of the Public Library system. Personally I feel I owe much to him for his help and counsel in those early years.

As a library pioneer his two great contributions are work with schools and Sunday opening.

Mr. Green's dominant trait was perseverance. Whether it was a baffling reference question to solve in his beloved Green Library; a baffling penny to be pursued up and down the columns of his account-book, or a baffling city council, plunged in materialism and heedless of the library's call for funds, — if there was any human way out, this unflinching librarian would not stay baffled long. In his preparation for a paper on the history of the local Unitarian parish, he had his secretary read aloud to him every scrap of manuscript record relating to the church, at an expense of hundreds of dreary hours.

As a writer Mr. Green employed a style of diction more properly called direct, forceful and unadorned, than conscious and graceful. "Rugged" might be its best descriptive adjective. With him writing was merely a means to secure a given end, and it is doubtful if he ever gave much thought to the language in which he clothed his ideas. His longer essays (for instance his sketch of Worcester libraries in the *Worcester County History*, 1889) are models of painstaking research and accurate expression.

Extending along the top of the fifteen-foot bookcase in the secluded chamber at the Worcester Library, still called "Mr. Green's room," is a row of some seventy cheerful red moroccos, comprising the publications of the *British Archaeological Journal* from its beginnings, in 1844, and forming a pleasant link in memory's chain that unites Mr. Green with his library. For next to his enthusiasm for the library book, in the hands of the right reader, came his passion for the spade of the archeologist, and never did he enjoy a vacation more than when pacing off a stretch of Hadrian's Wall in Northumberland, or following the lines of the Roman basilica at Uriconium. This systematic study of Roman remains in Britain, pursued with characteristic thoroughness during many years, furnished Mr. Green with a steady but spirited hobbyhorse to ride, in whose company he passed many happy hours, and through whose companionship he was always ready to speak *ex tempore* with knowledge and enthusiasm on an unhackneyed and entertaining topic.

SAMUEL SWETT GREEN

As a reader, Mr. Green could not be called omnivorous in the ordinary sense of one who consumes a vast amount of miscellaneous reading, and who is passionately devoted to its practice. Doubtless he would have been pleased to be included, with Dr. Billings, in that coterie, but his eyesight forbade. For many years, during the height of his activity, he was so handicapped by poor eyes, that he had to spend hours and even days at a time in a darkened room, and employed a secretary to read to him for two hours every morning before going to the library, while during library hours his assistants spent much time in reading aloud extracts and book-reviews. For one suffering from such a misfortune, even an approach to the vast amount of skimming and galloping through four hundred pages in an hour and a quarter, in the attempt to pluck the heart out of a book, as most librarians have to do, must have been quite unthinkable for him. How he ever accomplished what he did in familiarizing himself with the contents of books, seems almost miraculous. Take for example, the occasion, referred to in this essay, of inviting the public school teachers to the library for the book-talk on the literature of geography. Mr. Green said he would select "say one hundred" specimens for exhibition. Although he could not, in reason, have tried to evaluate any such number at one session, yet if he took only a half or a quarter, or even a tenth of that number, he would lay out for himself a task requiring a deal of rapid reading.

As an offset to his handicap of poor eyes, his memory was remarkably tenacious. Whatever he read or had read to him, was his for good, and the same might be said of any other facts definitely assimilated. For years he could tell you not only the book, but also the exact place on a page where he had met some interesting statement. In keeping his personal accounts, in which he was meticulously methodical, he would set down the amounts of expenditure in proper order, without indicating the items corresponding, but for weeks or months would keep them all mentally shelf-listed, and could thus fit item to amount, if needed. In his attitude toward the general public and readiness to give up his time to any questioner in the Green Library, he was most generous and democratic. In the main, he was at anybody's beck and call, almost without limitation of time. Toward elderly people he was always especially patient and considerate, treating them, whether friends or strangers, with the utmost respect and attention. Now and then this excellent practice of putting himself at everybody's service would cause some confusion, as when an old crony would come in for a little chat and sit down by the librarian's desk, which he kept in an open and unguarded corner of the Green Library; presently a loud guffaw might float out over the roller-top desk, requiring no amplifier to reach the astonished ears of high school pupils beyond.

In his *Memories of Travel* the late Lord Bryce tells a remarkable story of a retired major in the Austrian army who eked out a scanty pension by guiding small parties among the peaks of the Hungarian Alps. Starting out one morning with a troup of fat Viennese hotel-keepers, the old Major found much trouble in maintaining a proper mileage, and presently was informed of the imminence of a general strike unless water were forthcoming at once. "Have patience, my friends," the guide besought, "there is a refreshing spring round the next turn of the road." Loud therefore were the murmurs when the spring was found to be dry. "Do not yet despair," exclaimed the Major, casting a hasty but penetrating glance toward the heights beyond, "Moses-like, I will strike this rock, and promise you water within ten minutes." Grumbling and incredulous they sat down and were astounded to find, within five minutes, a tiny rivulet trickling down the dry bed, and before the expiration of the prescribed period, all had been able to slake their thirst. The Major's keen eye had noticed that the sun's rays, having just rounded the mountain's edge, were resting squarely on a great patch of snow, fallen during the night, so he staked his reputation on its melting in time. Thus did Green, Winsor, Dewey, Cutter and the other library Forty-niners strike that magic rock of faith in the Pennsylvania wilderness of '76, that we, librarians and public of this twentieth century, may drink copious and refreshing draughts.

With a power of delineation given to but few, Lytton Strachey, in his *Eminent Victorians* draws an indelible picture of Cardinal Manning, toward the end of his life. "When the guests were gone . . . he would bring out his diaries and his memoranda; he would arrange his notes; he would turn over again the yellow leaves of faded correspondences; seizing his pen he would pour out his comments and reflections, and fill, with an extraordinary solicitude, page after page with elucidations, explanations, justifications of the vanished incidents of a remote past."

Thus, in a way, but still quite differently, would Mr. Green, toward the end of his career, prepare his mind for reflection at the close of day. Drawing down and carefully locking the roller-top of his cherry desk, he would perch on the edge of his ample red leather-seated chair (so generous in width that like Dr. Holmes in Phillips Brooks's place, he was in some danger of "rattling round") and support his short legs on the well-worn hassock beneath. Then with his elbows on the chair-arms and hands lying on his lap, permitting now and then an asthmatic snuffle to escape, he would slip off his seal-ring, and twirl it gently between his fingers. Thus would he sit for long minutes at a time, planning out the next day's work or pondering on some knotty problem in his board. Unlike Cardinal Manning, on such occasions, Mr. Green never took a pen in hand, and cast his thoughts forward to the future, rather than backward to the past.

Among the archives of the Commonwealth of Massachusetts may be found the following articles of incorporation :

Be it known that, whereas Justin Winsor, C. A. Cutter, Samuel S. Green, James L. Whitney, Melvil Dewey, Fred B. Perkins and Thomas M. Bicknell have associated themselves with the intention of forming a corporation under the name of the "American Library Association" . . . now therefore, I, Henry B. Peirce, Secretary of the Commonwealth of Massachusetts, do hereby certify that [they] . . . are hereby made an existing corporation . . . this tenth day of December, in the year of Our Lord one thousand eight hundred and seventy-nine.

This is the roster of the charter members among our American library pioneers, a stanch and prophetic band, to whose original scroll no names, however worthy, can ever be added. While now and then, meteor-like, a Ford or a Burbank will burst upon the horizon and crash through the humdrum routine of everyday life, for the most part, our American frontiers, whether in exploration, in politics or librarianship, are pretty well leveled ; not many of us in this second generation of the growth of the American public library are slated for berths in the hall of fame.

EVENING — AFTERGLOW

A bit of retrospect, however, is good for us all, as we
tread the beaten path; even now we have an honor-
able past, and can look back with feelings of glowing
pride, to the careers of those pathfinders of '76 who
have made our work joyous and comfortable today.
Truly are we blest with a happy heritage; hats off to
our pioneers!

Appendix and Index

APPENDIX

I. Portraits

Two oil paintings of Mr. Green adorn the walls of the library. The first, a full-length likeness, painted by Walter Gilman Page, in 1892, was presented to the Board of Directors, in recognition of Mr. Green's services to the community, by a committee of twenty-three leading citizens, headed by Stephen Salisbury, Jr., with Andrew Haskell Green, "Father of Greater New York," signing last. The other, a bust portrait, was executed in 1905 or 1906 and is the work of an English artist, R. I. Paley. It gives the subject a rather melancholy cast of feature. The photograph used opposite page 19 is taken from Mr. Green's Harvard class-book of 1858, formerly owned by his classmate, Joseph A. Shaw.

Decidedly more pleasing as a work of art than either of the first two is a large portrait of Dr. John Green, founder of the Reference Library, by W. H. Furness, brother of the great Shakesperean scholar. A life-size plaster cast of the old doctor, by B. H. Kinney, a local sculptor, shows him seated in a chair, with his beloved books about him.

Quaintest of all is the lithograph engraving of old Dr. John Green, in his gig or "one hoss shay" of 1832, reproduced opposite page 10.

II. A. L. A. Conferences

As a pioneer in supporting organized librarianship, Mr. Green attended all the national conferences that were held from 1876 to 1894 inclusive, that is, fourteen, and eleven thereafter, a total of twenty-five, the last being appropriately at Pasadena, in 1911, just twenty years after his term as president.

III. Bibliography

(a) Author; arranged chronologically

Report of the Committee on the Library. 1870. p. 17–42.
Published in the eleventh annual report of the Library.

APPENDIX

The desirableness of establishing personal intercourse and relations between librarians and readers in popular libraries. 1876. 15 p.

Published also in *Library Journal* 1 : 74–81, 1876.

Special report of the Free public library of the city of Worcester, prepared for use at the International exhibition of 1876. 1876. 14 p.

Considerations concerning the desirability of having sensational fiction in public libraries, and some practical suggestions in regard to the regulation of the use of novels and stories for the young. 1879. 21 p.

Published also in *Library Journal* 4 : 345–55, 1879.

Report of the Committee on the distribution of public documents. *Library Journal* 6 : 86–90, 1881.

Aids and guides for readers. *Library Journal* 7 : 139–47, 1882.

Gleanings from the sources of the Second parish, Worcester. American antiquarian society. Proceedings n.s. 2 : 301–20,1883.

Libraries and schools; papers. 1883. 126 p.

Library aids; revised with references from Poole's *Index* and a chapter on "Books and articles on reading from Foster's *Libraries and readers.*" 1883. 129 p.

Public libraries and schools; results of recent efforts to make the former useful to the latter. Mass. Board of education. Annual report 1884 : 233–54.

Edward Jarvis, M.D. American antiquarian society. Proceedings n.s. 3 : 484–87, 1885.

Opening libraries on Sunday. *Sunday Review*, London, Jan. 1885 : 71–73.

Aaron Bancroft. *Christian Register*, May 27, 1886. Clippings. 3 p.

Pliny Earle Chase; a memoir. American antiquarian society. Proceedings n.s. 4 : 316–21, 1887.

Use of the voluntary system in the maintenance of ministers in the colonies of Plymouth and Massachusetts Bay. American antiquarian society. Proceedings n.s. 4 : 86–126, 1886.

APPENDIX

Bathsheba Spooner. American antiquarian society. Proceedings n.s. 5 : 430–36, 1888.

Industrial libraries. *Library Journal* 14 : 215–25, 1889.

Public libraries of Worcester. Hurd's History of Worcester county 2 : 1491–1509, 1889.

The duties of trustees and their relations to librarians. *Library Journal* 15, No. 12 : 24–27, 1890.

George Bancroft. American antiquarian society. Proceedings n.s. 7 : 237–56, 1891.

Some functions of a library; presidential address at San Francisco. *Library Journal* 16 : C1–9, 1891.

Adaptation of libraries to constituencies. U. S. Commissioner of education. Report 1892–3, 1 : 698–703.

Scotch-Irish in America. American antiquarian society. Proceedings n.s. 10 : 32–70, 1895.

Use of pictures in libraries. Mass. Free public library commission. 8th annual report 1897 : 17–28.

Inter-library loans in reference work. *Library Journal* 23 : 567–68, 1898.

How to encourage the foundation of libraries in small towns : remarks suggested by service on the Massachusetts free public library commission. *Library Journal* 24, No. 7 : 14–15, 1899.

Charles L. Nichols's Bibliography of Worcester, a criticism. *Library Journal* 25 : 597–98, 1900.

The Craigie house, Cambridge, during its occupancy by Andrew Craigie and his widow. American antiquarian society. Proceedings n.s. 13 : 312–52, 1900.

Memoir of Edward Griffin Porter. Colonial society of Massachusetts. Publications 7 : 55–62, 1900.

My first play. 1901? 7 p. mounted clippings.

Reminiscences of John Fiske. American antiquarian society. Proceedings n.s. 14 : 421–28, 1901.

Did Sir Thomas Browne write *Fragments on mummies?* American antiquarian society. Proceedings 15 : 442–47, 1903.

APPENDIX

Andrew Haswell Green — a sketch of his ancestry, life and work. American antiquarian society. Proceedings n.s. 16: 200–20, 1904.

Remarks on Elihu Burritt. American antiquarian society. Proceedings n.s. 16: 275–80, 1904.

Some of the Roman remains in England. American antiquarian society. Proceedings n.s. 18: 57–97, 1906.

Worcester, England, and Worcester, Mass. 1908. 40 p.

Remarks at the 50th anniversary of the founding of the Worcester free public library, December 23, 1909. p. 14–22. 1910.

The public library movement in the United States, 1853–1893; from 1876, reminiscences of the writer. 1913. 336 p.

Samuel Swett Green; some autobiographical sketches of incidents in his life. *Library Journal* 38: 666–70, 1913.

(*b*) Subject

Appreciation. *L'opinion Publique*, Supplement. Nov. 5, 1897. General article in local French newspaper.

Coombs, Z. W. Samuel Swett Green; memorial prepared for the Board of Directors, on his retirement, Jan. 1909. 18 p.

Crane, E. B., ed. Historic homes, institutions and memoirs of Worcester County, Mass. 1907. v. 1: 31–34.

Garver, A. S. Appreciation. *Worcester Magazine* 12: 36–37. 1909. Same article in *Library Journal* 34: 269–71, 1909.

The Green family. Carl's tour in Main street. 1889. p. 129–35.

Nutt, C. History of Worcester and its people. 1919. v. 3: 6–9.

Obituary notices and articles on Samuel Swett Green. *Worcester Telegram* and *Worcester Evening Gazette*. Dec. 9, 1918.

Samuel Swett Green: some autobiographical sketches of incidents in his life. *Library Journal* 38: 666–70, 1913.

Testimonial on Mr. Green's retirement as librarian, March 11, 1909; speeches, menu-card, circulars, etc.

INDEX

INDEX

Catalog, printed *vs.* card, 41.
Christian Citizen, E. Burritt's newspaper, 33.
Clark University, Mr. Green's connection with, 71.
Coombs, Zelotes W., speaks at Mr. Green's retiring dinner, 62.
Cross, Albert E., visits Worcester, England, 38–39.
Crosfield, Joseph, invents "Friendly international addresses," 1846, 33.
Crunden, Frederick M., with Mr. Green at Chicago, 1893, 46.
Cutter, Charles A.:
library pioneer, 76.
incorporator of A. L. A., 78.

Dana, John C., type of modern librarian, 72.
Decimal classification in Worcester Public Library, 1891, 49.
Dewey, Melvil, with Mr. Green at Chicago, 1893, 46.
inspects Worcester library, 51–53.
library pioneer, 76.
incorporator of A. L. A., 78.
Dole, Charles F., conducts Mr. Green's funeral services, 68.
Douglas (Play), attended by Mr. Green and uncle, 17.
Dudley, Mass., birthplace of Z. Baker, 24.

Edinburgh, Rotary conference at, 38.
Engler, Edmund A., speaker, 50th anniversary Worcester Public Library, 65.
Estes, Hiram C., praises Dr. Thomas Green, 7.
Exeter, England, ladies of, send friendly address to Philadelphia, 33.

Fletcher, William I., library pioneer, 72.

Forbes, William T., speaks at Mr. Green's retiring dinner, 61.
Forest Hills Crematory Chapel, 68.
Foster, William E., estimate of Mr. Green, 70–71.
Francis, George E., classmate of Mr. Green, 19.
"Free" defined in library parlance, 53.
Furness, William H., artist, 83.

Gardner, John L., classmate of Mr. Green, 19.
Garver, Austin S., promoted art interests, 41.
German librarianship, tendencies of, 47.
Green, Andrew H., "Father of Greater New York," 83.
Green, Elizabeth (Swett), *see* Mrs. James Green.
Green, James, 1802–1874:
father of Samuel S., 9.
career, 9–10.
ambitions for children's education, 11.
Green, Mrs. James, *d.* 1901, social gifts, 11–12.
Green, John, I, 1736–1799, career, 8–9.
Green, John, II, 1763–1808, career, 9.
Green, John, III, 1784–1865:
career, 9–10.
library, 10.
will and legacy, 10–11, 54.
takes nephew to theater, 17.
founds Worcester Public Library, 25.
portrait, 83.
Green, Samuel S.:
library atmosphere at time of his birth, 3.
born, February 20, 1837, 12.
shyness in boyhood, 13.
at Mrs. Heywood's Infant School, 13.
ambitious to emulate older brother, 13.
schooling, 13–15.
first idea of "school and library," 14.
enters Harvard College, 15.

[88]

INDEX

[89]

INDEX

INDEX

INDEX

INDEX

One thousand copies of this book were printed by
D. B. Updike, The Merrymount Press, Boston, in
April, 1926, of which five hundred are numbered.